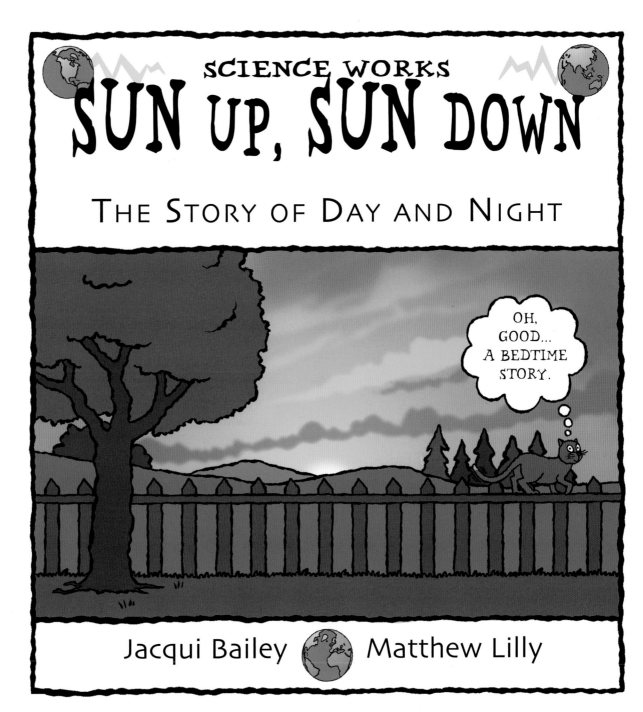

SCIENCE WORKS
SUN UP, SUN DOWN
THE STORY OF DAY AND NIGHT

OH, GOOD... A BEDTIME STORY.

Jacqui Bailey • Matthew Lilly

Picture Window Books • Minneapolis, Minnesota

First American edition published in 2004 by
Picture Window Books
A Capstone imprint
1710 Roe Crest Drive
North Mankato, MN 56003
www.capstonepub.com

First published in Great Britain by
A & C Black Publishers Limited
37 Soho Square, London W1D 3QZ
Copyright © Two's Company 2003

Library of Congress Cataloging-in-Publication Data
Bailey, Jacqui.
Sun up, sun down : the story of day and night / written by
Jacqui Bailey ; illustrated by Matthew Lilly.— 1st American ed.
p. cm. — (Science works)
Summary: Follows the sun from dawn to dusk to explain how
light rays travel, how shadows are formed, how the moon lights
up the night sky, and more.
Includes bibliographical references and index.
ISBN-13: 978-1-4048-0567-5 (library binding)
ISBN-10: 1-4048-0567-2 (library binding)
ISBN-13: 978-1-4048-1128-7 (paperback)
ISBN-10: 1-4048-1128-1 (paperback)
1. Earth—Rotation—Juvenile literature. 2. Day—Juvenile
literature. 3. Night—Juvenile literature. 4. Sun—Juvenile
literature. [1. Earth—Rotation. 2. Day. 3. Night. 4. Sun. 5. Moon.]
I. Lilly, Matthew, ill. II. Title.
QB633 .B35 2004
525'.35—dc22   2003020119

Printed in the United States of America at in Eau Claire, Wisconsin.
072018   000782

For Vickie
JB

For Oliver, Timothy, and Gregory
ML

Never look straight at the sun, even through sunglasses. The sun's light is so strong, it can seriously damage your eyes.

3

Special thanks to our advisers for their expertise:

Paul Ohmann, Ph.D., Assistant Professor of Physics
University of St. Thomas, St. Paul, Minnesota

Susan Kesselring, M.A., Literacy Educator
Rosemount-Apple Valley-Eagan (Minnesota) School District

5

The night sky was pitch black, and the yard was dark. It was long after midnight, and everything was quiet.

Most animals were fast asleep, curled up in holes and burrows and nests.

The family was fast asleep, too. A porch light was shining, but the rest of the house was dark and still.

ZZZzzz

zzzZZ

6

Then a breeze rustled the leaves of a tree. Behind the house, a strip of light appeared between the land and the sky.

The light became stronger and brighter, and pushed back the dark.

The sky changed from black to gray to blue. Streaks of sunlight raced across the land. The sun peeked over the horizon.

It was dawn—time to start another day.

Little by little, the sun rose in the sky, sending out its beams of light in lines called rays.

When the rays hit the yard, everything started warming up.

The damp grass steamed as it began to dry, and life suddenly got busier.

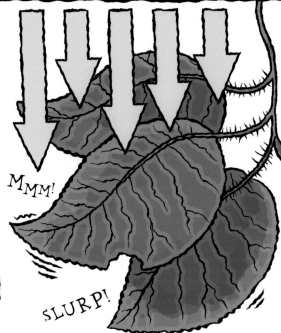

MMM!

SLURP!

Plants lifted up their leaves and greedily soaked up the sun's rays. It had been a long, dark night, and they needed the energy in the sunlight to make their food.

Insects uncurled and crawled into the sunshine. Other animals stretched and yawned. They were hungry, too.

OOOH, THAT'S BETTER. NOTHING LIKE A BIT OF SUNLIGHT TO START THE DAY.

MMM, BREAKFAST!

MMM, BREAKFAST!

Some chomped on plants. Some gobbled up insects . . .

. . . and some ate just about anything they could get their hands on!

MMM, BREAKFAST!

But imagine what would happen if the sun didn't rise.

Without its light and warmth, all the plants on Earth would starve and die.

If the plants died, the plant-eating animals would die, too.

And if the plant-eating animals died, there would be nothing for the other animals to eat, either.

Earth would be dark and cold and empty. It's lucky for us we have the sun!

The sun shines so strongly on us, you might think it was very close by. But it's not. It's millions and millions of miles away.

The reason we can see and feel it from so far away is that the sun itself is incredibly bright and hot. It's so hot that it's impossible to get anywhere near the sun and survive! Scientists have taken close-up photographs of it, though.

RUMBLE!

RUMBLE!

BOOM!

BOOM!

RUMBLE!

RUMBLE!

BOOM!

They've discovered the sun is a gigantic ball of super-hot gases. Deep inside it, billions of explosions are taking place every second. These explosions create all that raging heat and light.

The sun was giving out other types of rays, too.

As well as light that we can see, the sun gives out light we can't see or feel, such as X-rays and ultraviolet light. These rays can be harmful to life on Earth.

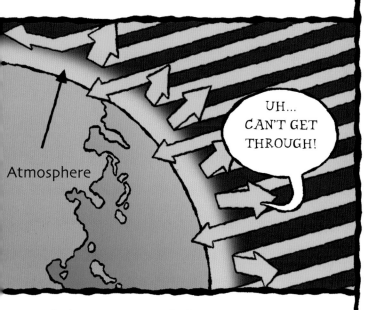

Atmosphere

Luckily, many of them are blocked out by the Earth's atmosphere— the layer of gases that covers Earth. But some harmful rays do get through.

So the children covered themselves with sunscreen to help block out harmful rays that might damage their skin.

13

With the sun overhead, it was hard to find anywhere shady and cool in the yard.

The family put up a big umbrella and sat in its shadow.

Light rays can pass through materials you can see through, such as glass and clear plastic.

Things you can't see through, such as wood or stone, block out light rays. A shadow appears on the other side of them.

All kinds of things make shadows on sunny days—houses, trees, fences, flower pots, and you! But shadows are always changing.

1 In the morning, when the sun is low in the sky, shadows are long.

2 As the sun climbs higher, shadows get shorter.

3 When the sun is at its highest, there are almost no shadows at all.

4 In the afternoon, shadows get long again—but this time they are on the other side!

It was sweltering in the afternoon heat, but the sun didn't stay high overhead.

It gradually swung to the other side of the sky and slid toward the land.

IS IT SUPPER TIME YET?

Slowly the shadows lengthened, and the sky grew darker.

I THINK I'LL HAVE AN EARLY NIGHT!

Most of the animals in the neighborhood (and the family) got ready to go to sleep. But not all! Some liked the dark and coolness of evening. For them, it was the best time to find their food.

EEEEK!

As the sun sank into the ground, the last bits of sunlight glowed orange and red in the sky.

Then the sun was gone. The sky was black, and it was nighttime again.

But hang on a minute—the sun hadn't really gone into the ground . . . had it?

Well, no, it hadn't. And the sun hadn't moved across the sky, either. That was just how it looked. In fact, it was Earth that had moved, but you'd have to have been in a spaceship to see it!

From a spaceship, you would see Earth as a bright, beautiful ball, hanging in the blackness of space.

But it's not just hanging there–it's moving all the time. It's spinning around and around, just like a giant spinning top.

As Earth spins, half of it is turned away from the sun. The sun's light doesn't reach it, so for this side, it's nighttime.

ZZZZZZZZ

The spinning doesn't make us dizzy because Earth never, ever changes its speed or the direction in which it spins. And we're so used to it, we don't feel a thing!

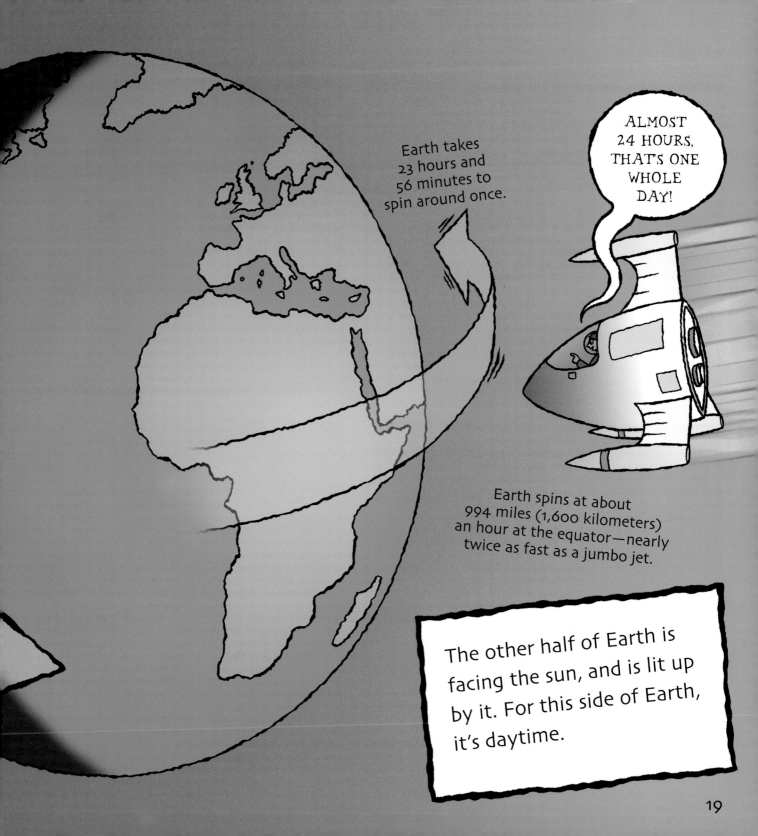

1 So at dawn, when the sun rose over the yard, this part of Earth was just turning toward the sun.

2 At noon, the yard was face to face with the sun.

3 When it was evening in the yard, this part of Earth was turning away from the sun.

4 At midnight, the yard was facing away from the sun. It was in Earth's shadow.

But even though it was nighttime in the yard, the sky wasn't entirely black. A glowing lantern of light hung there. It was the moon.

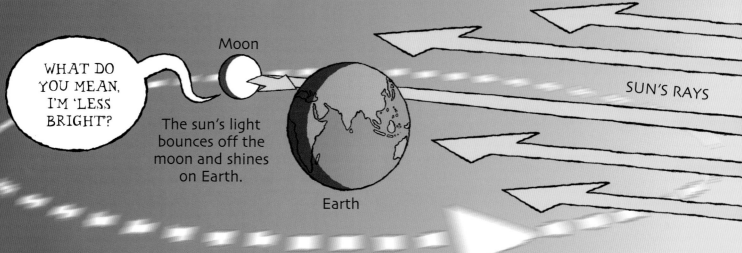

WHAT DO YOU MEAN, I'M 'LESS BRIGHT'?

Moon

The sun's light bounces off the moon and shines on Earth.

Earth

SUN'S RAYS

The moon is far less bright than the sun because the moon doesn't make any light of its own. It's a lifeless ball of rock. It only shines because the sun's light is bouncing off it.

The moon is our closest neighbor in space. It travels around and around Earth—just as Earth goes around the sun.

Yep! It's true. Earth moves in two completely different ways. As well as spinning around on itself, it's also traveling in circles (well, sort of egg-shaped circles) around the sun! This huge, looping journey is called an orbit.

DON'T YOU GUYS EVER GET TIRED OF DOING THE SAME OLD THING?

It takes Earth 365.25 days to make one complete orbit of the sun. That's one whole year.

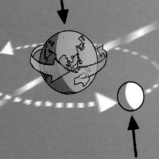

The moon orbits Earth while Earth orbits the sun.

Earth's orbit is 595 million miles (958 million kilometers) long, and Earth zips around it at 67,000 miles (108,000 kilometers) per hour—that's almost four times the speed of a space shuttle!

Earth never stops or slows down. It's been orbiting the sun for about 4½ billion years, and it will keep going for billions more.

And do you know what the really amazing thing is?
Earth's orbit is exactly the right distance from the sun!

Any closer, and Earth would get too hot. The oceans would dry up, and the world would be an empty desert.

Any farther away, and Earth would get too cold. Everything would be frozen solid.

But Earth is not too close or too far away. We have just the right amount of heat and light for plants and animals—including us—to live.

And that's nearly the end of the story . . . but not quite.
The moon wasn't the only light in the night sky. There were also hundreds, even thousands, of tiny, twinkling pinpricks of light. They were stars!

WOW! LOOK AT ALL THOSE STARS!

Even the stars aren't really the way they look from Earth.
Those tiny, twinkling lights are billions upon billions of miles away, and each one of them is a gigantic, glowing, scorchingly hot sun, like our own.

You never know—maybe one of those faraway suns has a world going around it that's just like Earth.

And maybe someone is sitting on that planet, too, reading about their sun!

WHICH IS BIGGEST?

From Earth, the sun and the moon look about the same size. But the moon is really only a quarter of the size of Earth, whereas the sun is more than 100 times bigger!

So if Earth were the size of a cherry pit, then the sun would be as big as a beach ball, and the moon would be almost as small as a pinhead!

I'M SCARED!

HOW FAR?

ZOOOMMM!

PUFF! PANT!

The sun is 93 million miles (150 million kilometers) from Earth. If you climbed in a car and drove there at 60 miles (97 kilometers) per hour, it would take you about 177 years to arrive—though the heat from the sun would fry you to a crisp long before you got there!

Sunlight travels much, much faster than that. It takes a little more than eight minutes for a ray of sunlight to get from the sun to the surface of Earth.

MOVING AROUND

No matter where you live on Earth, the sun always rises more or less in the east and sets more or less in the west. If you live in the northern half of the world, the sun moves across the southern half of your sky. If you live in the southern half of the world, the sun moves across the northern half of the sky.

Exactly where you see the sun rise or set also depends on what time of year it is. In winter, the sun is lower in the sky than in summer, even at noon. It rises later and sets earlier, too.

Noon in summer

Noon in winter

Sunrise

Sunset

GIANTS AND DWARFS

Even stars don't last forever. One day, about 5 billion years from now, our sun will start to go out.

To begin with, it will swell up, growing as much as 100 times bigger. It will become what scientists call a red giant. Hopefully, by this time people will have moved somewhere else, as Earth will be burned to ashes.

Then the sun will start to shrink. Over millions more years, it will turn into a small white star about the size of Earth. Scientists call this a white dwarf. After this, our sun will slowly fade away.

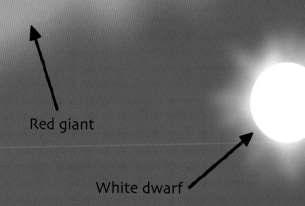

Red giant

White dwarf

TRY IT AND SEE

SUN TIME

Thousands of years ago, before we invented clocks and watches, people used the sun to help them measure time. They did it by making something called a sundial.

OH GOOD, IT'S TIME FOR LUNCH.

Try making your own sundial. It will take most of a day, so choose a time when you don't have to be anywhere special—and when the sun is shining!

You will need:
- a large sheet of white cardboard or paper
- some modeling clay
- a wooden stick, such as a pencil
- a pen and a ruler
- an alarm clock

1 Choose a good spot to make your sundial. It needs to be outside in the open where no shadows will fall on it as the day goes by—and where it won't be moved.

2

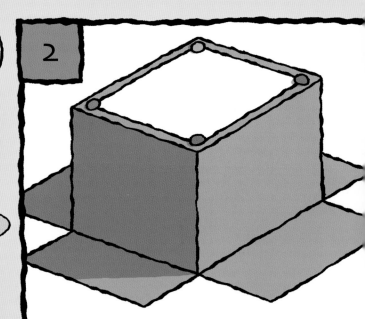

Put the sheet of paper or cardboard on a firm, flat surface—such as a table, the sidewalk, or even an upside-down tray or cardboard box.

Put a stone on each corner to hold it in place.

3 Use the modeling clay to make a base for the wooden stick. Make sure the stick will stand upright. Then place the stick and the base in the middle of your paper. Draw a circle around the base to mark its position, and don't move it.

   The stick is called the gnomon (NO-mon). When the sun shines on it, the gnomon will make a shadow on the paper.

4 Start as early as you can in the morning. Set your alarm clock to go off every hour during the day so you don't forget. Each time the alarm goes off, check the position of the shadow on the paper, and draw a line along it with the pen and ruler. Write the time you drew the line next to it.

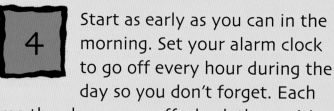

By the end of the day, you will have made a sundial. The next day, compare the gnomon's shadow to the lines you drew. You can use your sundial to find out the time without looking at a clock—as long as the sun is shining!

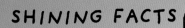

SHINING FACTS

*BRIGHT...
YET VERY
SLOW.*

The sun's light may
only take about
eight minutes to
get to Earth,
but the energy
that creates it
takes more than
a million years to
get from the center
of the sun to its surface.

*THIS
COULD TAKE
SOME TIME.*

The distance from one star to another
is so huge that scientists measure distance
in space in "light-years." One light-year is
the distance traveled by a light ray in one
year—which is 5,900 billion miles
(9,500 billion kilometers)!

The surface of the sun seems
smooth from a distance, but it is
always bubbling with energy.
Every now and then, huge flares of
hot gas spurt out into space. They
can stretch for thousands of
miles before falling
back to the sun.

INDEX

FACT HOUND

Fact Hound offers a safe, fun way to find Web sites related to this book. All of the sites on Fact Hound have been researched by our staff.

1. Visit www.facthound.com

2. Type in this special code: 1404805672

3. Click the FETCH IT button.

   Your trusty Fact Hound will fetch the best sites for you!